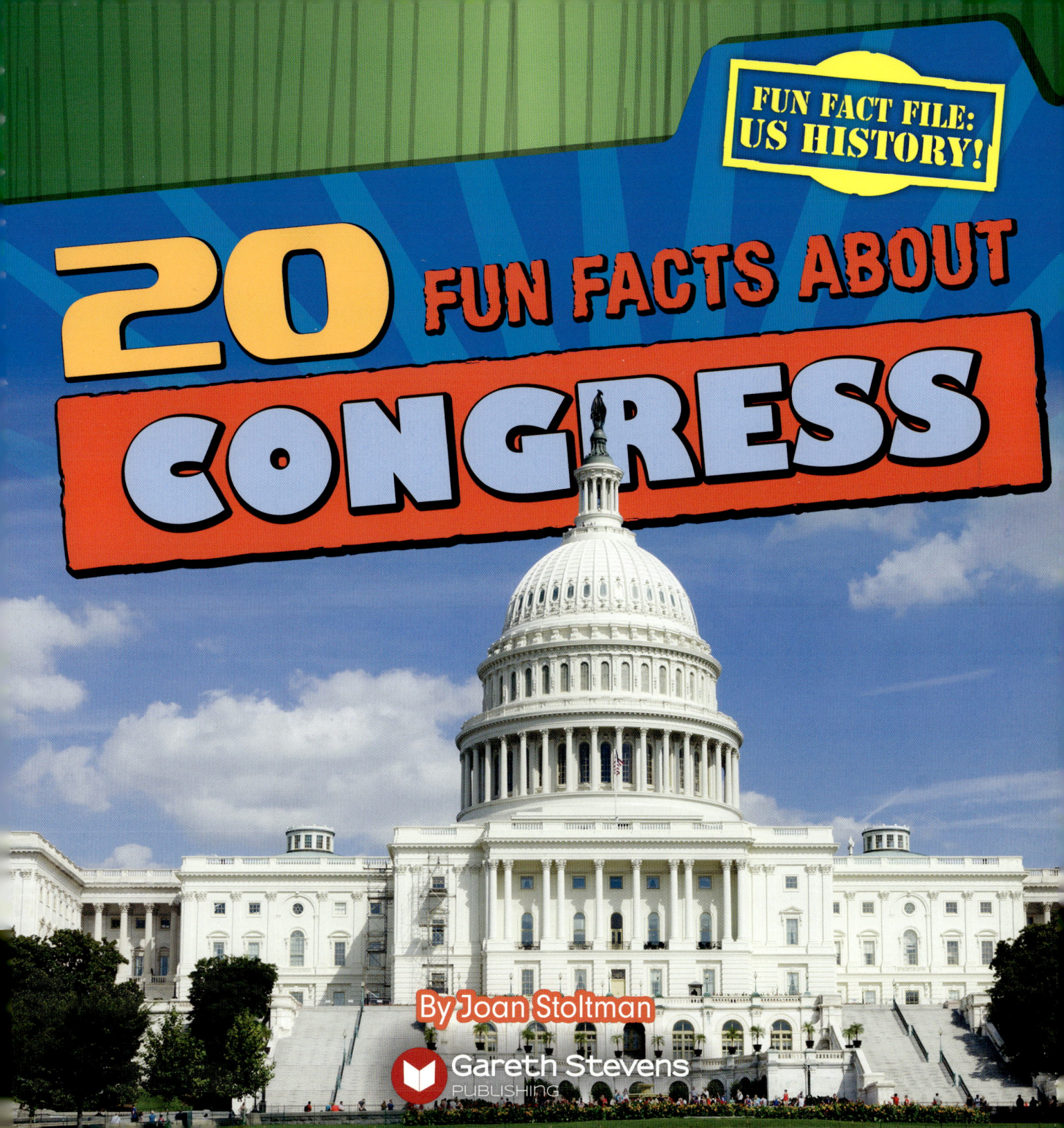

FUN FACT FILE: US HISTORY!

20 FUN FACTS ABOUT CONGRESS

By Joan Stoltman

Gareth Stevens
PUBLISHING

Please visit our website, www.garethstevens.com. For a free color catalog of all our high-quality books, call toll free 1-800-542-2595 or fax 1-877-542-2596.

Library of Congress Cataloging-in-Publication Data

Names: Stoltman, Joan, author.
Title: 20 fun facts about Congress / Joan Stoltman.
Description: New York : Gareth Stevens Publishing, 2019. | Series: Fun fact file: US history! | Includes index.
Identifiers: LCCN 2017058474| ISBN 9781538219010 (library bound) | ISBN 9781538218990 (pbk.) | ISBN 9781538219003 (6 pack)
Subjects: LCSH: United States. Congress–Juvenile literature.
Classification: LCC JK1025 .S76 2019 | DDC 328.73–dc23
LC record available at https://lccn.loc.gov/2017058474

Published in 2019 by
Gareth Stevens Publishing
111 East 14th Street, Suite 349
New York, NY 10003

Copyright © 2019 Gareth Stevens Publishing

Designer: Sarah Liddell
Editor: Mariel Bard

Photo credits: Cover, p. 1 Konstantin L/Shutterstock.com; p. 5 Photo courtesy of Photographs in the Carol M. Highsmith Archive, Library of Congress, Prints and Photographs Division; p. 6 Scewing/Wikimedia Commons; p. 7 Psychless/Wikimedia Commons; pp. 8, 15 (David Yulee) Davepape/Wikimedia Commons; p. 9 (Augustus Dodge) Amgisseman/ Wikimedia Commons; p. 9 (Henry Dodge) Dark Attsios/Wikimedia Commons; p. 10 P. S. Burton/Wikimedia Commons; p. 11 Alex Wong/Staff/Getty Images News/Getty Images; pp. 12, 27 Bettmann/Contributor/Bettmann/Getty Images; p. 13 MB298/Wikimedia Commons; p. 14 Mark Reinstein/Contributor/Corbis News/Getty Images; p. 15 (Andrew Butler) MarmadukePercy/Wikimedia Commons; p. 16 Centpacrr/Wikimedia Commons; pp. 17, 24 Photo courtesy of Library of Congress; p. 18 Terry Ashe/Contributor/The LIFE Images Collection/Getty Images; p. 19 JIM WATSON/Staff/AFP/Getty Images; p. 21 (medal) Nyctc7/Wikimedia Commons; p. 21 (Rosa Parks) Nard the Bard/Wikimedia Commons; p. 22 (Shirley Chisholm) Don Hogan Charles/Contributor/Archive Photos/Getty Images; p. 22 (Jeannette Rankin) Americus55/Wikimedia Commons; p. 23 GRuban/Wikimedia Commons; p. 25 The New York Historical Society/Contributor/Archive Photos/Getty Images; p. 26 Howcheng/Wikimedia Commons; p. 29 Druffeller/Wikimedia Commons.

Printed in the United States of America

CPSIA compliance information: Batch #CS18GS: For further information contact Gareth Stevens, New York, New York at 1-800-542-2595.

Contents

Words in the glossary appear in **bold** type the first time they are used in the text.

The House and the Senate

The United States Congress was created in 1789 under the highest law in the United States, the Constitution. Congress is the legislative, or lawmaking, branch of our government. It's made up of the Senate and the House of **Representatives**. The people in each state vote for two senators. They also vote for their representatives in the House. The number of representatives a state has depends on how many people live there.

Congress is one of the oldest legislatures in the world! Since 1789, many interesting—and sometimes weird—things have happened there!

Congress first met in 1789 in New York, New York. In 1790, it moved to Philadelphia, Pennsylvania. Today, Congress meets in the Capitol Building in Washington, DC, where it's been located since 1800.

The One and Only!

Only one person has served as a senator *after* serving as president.

Andrew Johnson was elected vice president in 1864 and became president after Abraham Lincoln was killed in 1865. Johnson served as president until 1869.

He was elected to the Senate in 1875, but died soon after.

John Quincy Adams is the only person to serve in the House after serving as president. He was president from 1825 to 1829. He was elected to the House in 1831 and served for nearly 17 years!

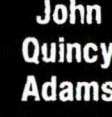

John Quincy Adams

Only one senator has ever represented three states during their political career.

Senator James Shields represented Illinois from 1849 to 1855. He served in Minnesota from 1858 until 1859. Shields also represented Missouri for 3 months in 1879!

James Shields

David Broderick is the only senator to be killed in a fight while in office.

Judge David Terry and Senator Broderick didn't agree about slavery. They said mean things about each other, and Terry challenged the senator to a gunfight to be held on September 13, 1859. During the fight, Terry shot Broderick, who died 3 days later.

David Broderick

All in the Family

Some people have served in Congress with their parents!

Wisconsin senator Henry Dodge and his son, Iowa senator Augustus Dodge, served in the Senate at the same time during the mid-1800s. Ohio representatives Frances and Oliver Bolton are the only mother and son to serve in Congress at the same time.

The Dodges served together from 1848 until Augustus resigned, or left the job, in 1855. Henry **retired** in 1857.

Augustus Dodge

Henry Dodge

9

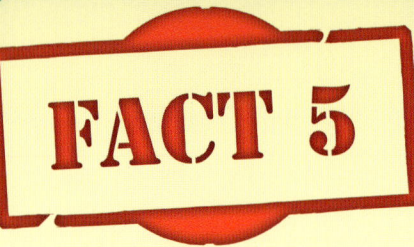

FACT 5

Two brothers were part of the very first House!

Pennsylvania representatives John Peter Gabriel Muhlenberg and Frederick Augustus Conrad Muhlenberg served together during the 1st and 3rd Congresses. Frederick was also the first Speaker of the House, which is the highest position in the House of Representatives.

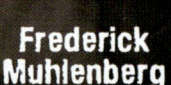

Frederick Muhlenberg

Loretta Sanchez

Linda Sanchez

The opening day of the 108th Congress on January 7, 2003, was historic for the Sanchez sisters.

FACT 6

Loretta and Linda Sanchez were the first sisters to serve in Congress at the same time.

When Linda was elected in 2003, the siblings made history. With both sisters representing California in the House, their **terms** overlapped from the 108th Congress through the 114th Congress.

FACT 7

More than 670 members of Congress have served in both the Senate and the House.

Most of these people have been men. As of December 2017, only 12 women have served as both senators and representatives so far.

Margaret Chase Smith became the first woman to serve in both houses of Congress when she won a Senate spot to represent Maine in 1948.

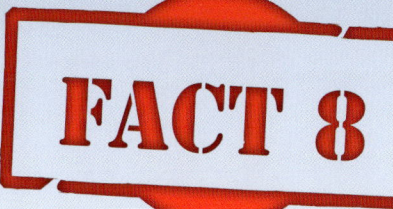

FACT 8

There are 28 people in history who have served as representatives for over 40 years!

Both senators and representatives can be reelected again and again. A senator serves for 6 years, but a representative's term lasts only 2 years. To serve in the House for 40 years means they'd have to win 20 elections!

John David Dingell Jr. holds the record for the longest-serving representative. He served from 1955 until 2015—that's 60 years!

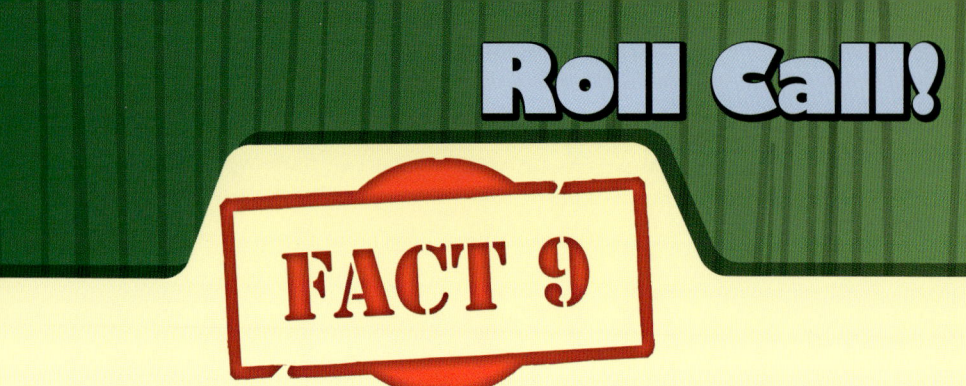

FACT 9

In the past, representatives could stop a vote from happening by pretending to be absent, or not there.

The rules used to say that half the representatives plus one needed to be present to allow for a vote. If enough representatives stayed silent during **roll call** and were marked "absent," a vote couldn't happen!

The trick for stopping a vote from happening was called a "disappearing **quorum**."

Senators David Yulee and Andrew Butler first used the disappearing quorum in the Senate in January 1851.

Andrew Butler

David Yulee

FACT 10

A disappearing quorum once led to 101 roll calls in the House in one day!

The only way to end a disappearing quorum was to do roll call over and over until enough people gave up and said they were present.

When someone tried to end the use of the disappearing quorum, some people banged their fists on tables!

On January 29, 1890, Speaker of the House Thomas Brackett Reed began marking silent representatives as "present but not voting" instead of "absent." But some congressmen didn't like that and fought back!

Thomas Bracket Reed wanted to make changes so that the House would stop avoiding votes and finally get things done.

Take Me Out to the Ball Game!

Congress has baseball teams!

Members of Congress have played a baseball game against each other most years since 1909. As of 2017, the two main political parties, the Republicans and the Democrats, have each won 39 games.

Pennsylvania representative John Tener was a professional baseball player before he was elected to Congress. It was his idea for Congress to have a yearly baseball game!

FACT 13

The phone book and family recipes have been read aloud in Congress.

In 1935, Senator Huey Long filibustered for 15 hours and 30 minutes by reading off family recipes. Filibustering means talking for so long that a vote must be moved to another day. The rule was you couldn't stop talking or leave the room.

Alfonse D'Amato

In 1986, Representative Alfonse D'Amato filibustered for 23 hours and 30 minutes by reading the local phone book out loud!

Strom Thurmond was also the oldest person to ever serve in the Senate. He retired in January 2003—just 1 month after turning 100 years old!

FACT 14

In 1957, Senator Strom Thurmond filibustered for 24 hours and 18 minutes!

Thurmond holds the record for the longest filibuster by one person. In case he needed to pee, Thurmond arranged for someone to wait with a bucket in a nearby coat closet!

Congressional Gold Medals for Presidents and First Ladies

NAME	YEAR	NO. PRESIDENT
George Washington	1776	1st president
Andrew Jackson	1815	7th president
Zachary Taylor	1846, 1847, 1848	12th president
Ulysses S. Grant	1863	18th president
Harry S. Truman	1984	33rd president
Lady Bird Johnson	1984	36th First Lady
Gerald R. and Betty Ford	1998	38th president and First Lady
Ronald and Nancy Reagan	2000	40th president and First Lady

Since the American Revolution, Congressional Gold Medals have been given out as a form of thanks to people who do great things for the United States. At least 290 representatives and 67 senators must agree on who gets one. A person or a group can receive the honor.

Congressional Gold Medals for Famous People

NAME	YEAR	CLAIM TO FAME
Charles A. Lindbergh	1928	first to fly a plane alone nonstop across the Atlantic Ocean
Thomas A. Edison	1928	inventor
Walt Disney	1968	creator of Mickey Mouse and cofounder of the Walt Disney Company
Roberto Clemente	1973	Puerto Rican baseball player and humanitarian
Jesse Owens	1988	African American runner and Olympic gold medalist
Frank Sinatra	1997	singer
Nelson Mandela	1998	former president of South Africa
Rosa Parks	1999	leader during the civil rights movement
Charles M. Schulz	2000	artist and creator of Charlie Brown
Jackie Robinson	2003	African American baseball player
Dr. Martin Luther King Jr. and Coretta Scott King	2004	leaders during the civil rights movement

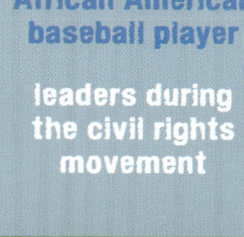

Rosa Parks

Awesome Women

FACT 15

In 1968, Shirley Chisholm became the first African American woman elected to Congress.

Chisolm was nicknamed "Fighting Shirley" because she fought hard for the people she represented. She was also the first black **candidate** for president!

Jeannette Rankin

Shirley Chisholm

Jeannette Rankin became the first woman to serve in Congress in 1916—4 years before women won the right to vote.

FACT 16

Forty-six women have served in Congress after their husband's death.

A **widow** would sometimes take over her husband's seat to finish out his term or until another man was given the seat. This has happened seven times in California, which is more than any other state!

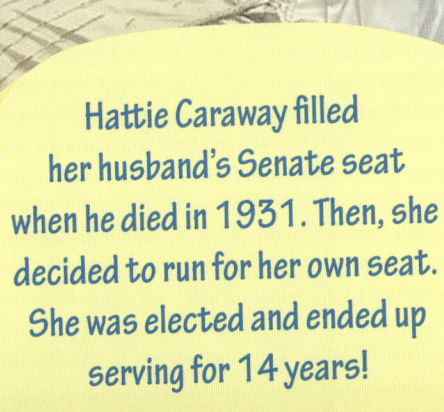

Hattie Caraway filled her husband's Senate seat when he died in 1931. Then, she decided to run for her own seat. She was elected and ended up serving for 14 years!

Fight!

FACT 17

A fight broke out in the House in January 1798!

Roger Griswold and Matthew Lyon hadn't been getting along in Congress. One day, Griswold attacked Lyon with a cane. Lyon reached for a nearby metal fire poker to hit Griswold back!

The fight began because a few weeks earlier, Lyon had spit in Griswold's face after being **offended** by him.

Brooks's fans mailed him canes to show their thanks and support for what he had done to Sumner, but he also had to pay a fine for the attack.

FACT 18

Senator Charles Sumner spent 3 years in the hospital recovering from a fight!

Preston Brooks and Laurence Keitt were offended when Charles Sumner spoke against a proslavery bill in 1856. Brooks beat Sumner with a cane while Keitt held back the crowd.

William Barksdale's wig fell off during a fight in the House, and everyone started laughing!

No one knew Barksdale was bald, and he tried to quickly hide under his wig—but hc put it on backward! This funny moment brought a quick end to the February 1858 fight.

Laurence Keitt

This fight was started by South Carolina representative Laurence Keitt. Keitt had taken part in the attack on Charles Sumner 2 years earlier.

The British set much of Washington, DC, on fire during the War of 1812.

FACT 20

The British held a fake session of Congress to make fun of America's government.

In 1814, during the War of 1812, the British attacked the Capitol. During their pretend congressional session, they voted to burn down the building. Thankfully, rain stopped the fire from destroying the building completely!

27

Visiting Congress

One of the best ways to learn about Congress is to visit Washington, DC, and see it for yourself! The Capitol Visitor Center, which opened in 2008, is a great place to start. You can take a tour of the Capitol Building, and you can even watch real, live sessions of the House and the Senate—just ask your parents to contact your members of Congress to get free passes.

There's so much more to learn about the Senate and the House of Representatives. Maybe someday you'll run for office and be part of Congress's amazing history!

The Capitol Visitor Center

The Capitol Visitor Center is located in front of the Capitol Building. It's almost as big as the Capitol itself!

Glossary

candidate: a person who runs in an election

civil rights movement: a time period in US history starting in the 1950s during which African Americans fought for equal civil rights, or the freedoms granted by law

humanitarian: one who works for the health and happiness of other people

offend: to cause a person to feel hurt, angry, or upset by something said or done by another

quorum: the smallest number of people who need to be present for decisions to be made

representative: one whose job in government is to represent, or stand for, a group of people

retire: to leave a job and stop working

roll call: the act of saying each name on a list to find out who is present

term: a period of time that an elected official can serve

widow: a woman whose husband has died

For More Information

Books

Hillard, Stephane. *The U.S. Capitol: The History of U.S. Congress.* New York, NY: PowerKids Press, 2018.

Krieg, Katherine. *Congress.* Vero Beach, FL: Rourke Educational Media, 2015.

Nelson, Robin, and Sandy Donovan. *The Congress: A Look at the Legislative Branch.* Minneapolis, MN: Lerner Publications, 2012.

Reis, Ronald A. *The US Congress for Kids: Over 200 Years of Lawmaking, Deal-Breaking, and Compromising.* Chicago, IL: Chicago Review Press, 2014.

Websites

Mapping Congress
history.house.gov/Map/Mapping-Congress/
This awesome interactive map of the United States breaks down facts about members of Congress by state.

Congress for Kids
www.congressforkids.net/
Learn all about the American government system.

US Capitol Visitor Center
www.visitthecapitol.gov/
Plan a visit to the Capitol to see where Congress works.

Index